Museums in the Life of a City

STRATEGIES FOR COMMUNITY PARTNERSHIPS

American Association of Museums
1995

Museums in the Life of a City: Strategies for Community Partnerships

Museums in the Life of a City project director: Portia Hamilton-Sperr
Editor: Ellen Cochran Hirzy
Consultants: Jim Zien and Alan Bell, Public Placemakers

Parts of this book were originally published as *Museums in the Life of a City: A Report from the Philadelphia Initiative for Cultural Pluralism* (1992).

Published by the American Association of Museums
© 1995 American Association of Museums.

ISBN 0-931201-21-7

American Association of Museums
1225 Eye St. N.W., Suite 200
Washington, D.C. 20005
202/289–1818

Endsheets: A community program at the Pennsylvania Academy of the Fine Arts, Museum of American Art.
Photo: Jonathan Wilson

Contents

Introduction

THE AMERICAN ASSOCIATION OF MUSEUMS experienced a landmark year in 1989 in its commitment to assist museums in their roles as educational institutions. Under the leadership of Joel Bloom, then the association's president, AAM formed a task force that ultimately produced the first major policy statement on the educational role of museums, *Excellence and Equity: Education and the Public Dimension of Museums*. During the same year, with the generous support of the Pew Charitable Trusts and in collaboration with Partners for Livable Places (now Partners for Livable Communities) and the Philadelphia museum community, the association began a process that resulted in Museums in the Life of a City: The Philadelphia Initiative for Cultural Pluralism.

The confluence of these two undertakings, while not deliberately planned, resulted in AAM's renewed commitment to guide museums in the complex process of institutional change. For both *Excellence and Equity* and Museums in the Life of a City were about change—changing the way museums approach their all-important role as educational institutions that serve their communities.

The pilot projects of the Philadelphia initiative demonstrate that it is possible, with dedication and collegiality, for museums and community-based organizations to work toward greater equity in their relationships and, ultimately, toward change. Museums can bring diverse points of view together in a dialogue. They can allow for a free flow of information and opinions, and they can be a place from which new information and ideas emerge.

Even in the toughest economic climate, the Philadelphia museum community attempted to realize its role in the educational, social, and economic life of a great city. The forces at work on cultural institutions in cities at times seem daunting, and yet museums as particular types of cultural institutions can have an effect on how communities share ideas and values.

With this publication, the association gives other museum professionals the benefit of what our colleagues in Philadelphia learned about forming partnerships with community organizations. The experiences, ideas, and strategies described in the following pages will, we hope, help museums begin the necessary steps to build bridges toward fuller realization of their public service role.

Prologue

Portia Hamilton-Sperr

THE MUSEUMS IN THE LIFE OF A CITY initiative did not fall conveniently into a beginning, a middle, and an end. It was an experiment—a probe—seen against the larger context of contemporary American events and shifting attitudes. In the early 1980s the word "racism" was rarely uttered in the discussion of museums. Yet when we wrote our project proposal in 1989, we spoke of our goal being to enhance "the appreciation of cultural diversity and to reduce prejudice and racism." We spoke of "building flexible museum-community partnerships and encouraging civic pride, better understanding of peoples and cultures, and an expanded community involvement with our city's museums."

This publication traces the steps in our experiment, from concept through evaluation, including the participants' thoughtful reflections on the impact of our efforts. The initiative began as a discussion among representatives of a variety of Philadelphia museums who came together in the summer of 1988 at the invitation of Joel N. Bloom, then president of the American Association of Museums and president of the Franklin Institute Science Museum. The hope was to create a project that would test ideas for building bridges between museums and their communities.

Under the auspices of AAM and in cooperation with Partners for Livable Places, the group received funding in 1990 from The Pew Charitable Trusts for Museums in the Life of a City: The Philadelphia Initiative for Cultural Pluralism. Under a regranting program administered by a small office in the city, cultural institutions and community-based arts and social service organizations would work together on one-year pilot projects.

The first year was devoted to gathering information, developing a management structure, and starting to build coalitions between Philadelphia museums and community organizations. We defined "community" as the nonmajority categories used in the 1990 U.S. Census, considering these to represent people who have borne the brunt of discrimination by the American mainstream for long periods: African Americans, Latinos, Asian Americans, and Native Americans. "Museums" were broadly defined to include libraries, a zoo, and historical organizations.

During the next two years we launched eleven pilot partnerships, built an information clearinghouse, presented public programs, produced an occasional newsletter, and conducted a Future Search Conference on cultural pluralism. Partners for Livable Places held a national conference in Philadelphia to focus on issues with which we and others across the country have been involved. Throughout the initiative, an executive committee representing fourteen museums and community organizations provided general guidance. Robert Sorrell, president of the Urban League of Philadelphia, and Joel Bloom chaired the committee.

In late 1994, two years after the pilot projects had been completed, the participants reflected on their experiences during focus groups convened by AAM. Their thoughtful observations about the initiative—the risks and benefits, disappointments and satisfactions, joys and frustrations—suggest that cultural institutions and community organizations in diverse urban areas like Philadelphia can indeed join forces to address some pressing needs.

Our initiative was carried out in the spirit of dialogue, a word that suggests the courtesy of listening, of responding, perhaps of questioning and disagreeing. It implies a respect for others and an expression of ideas in an atmosphere of trust. This book is its own kind of dialogue, presenting the words of those who were part of the action during the Museums in the Life of a City initiative.

Exploring the Possibilities

Ann Mintz

HOW CAN MUSEUMS PLAY A LARGER ROLE in the social fabric of the community? And, by extension, what social issues might museums be able to help address? The Museums in the Life of a City initiative started with these questions.

When representatives of Philadelphia museums held their first meetings, we set two ambitious goals: to identify the most important problems facing our city and to discuss ways that museums might make a contribution to their solution.

With striking candor and openness, those of us who were involved discussed at length a range of important but divisive issues: drugs and associated crime, housing and the homeless, children at risk, unemployment, racial and political fragmentation, the city's rich but underappreciated resources for cultural pluralism, funding cutbacks, the importance of education (including lifelong learning), museums' responsibility to families and communities, and even the need to find ways to promote civic pride and a sense of place by attacking blight and litter. We debated these issues within the context of the strengths of museums and their ability to make a difference.

We set two ambitious goals: to identify the most important problems facing our city and to discuss ways that museums might make a contribution to their solution.

"Museums are not in the business of social work," was one participant's comment. We agreed, however, that while there are many urban problems with which museums are unable to deal, museums are indeed *social agencies.* There are, for instance, areas in which museums are particularly expert, such as education and the promotion of community pride. There are

We agreed that while there are many urban problems with which museums are unable to deal, museums are indeed social agencies. There are, for instance, areas in which museums are particularly expert, such as education and the promotion of community pride.

other issues, like racial and ethnic divisions, in which they could play a constructive role. "Culture," said another participant, "is at the center of the healing of the country."

We explored many possibilities and concluded that the unique strength of museums lay in the presentation, interpretation, and celebration of cultural pluralism. Philadelphia is famous as a city of neighborhoods, a multiracial patchwork of discrete communities. Philadelphians identify passionately with their neighborhoods and their ethnic groups. But we noted that this identification can also lead to fragmentation, even conflict.

Museums, we decided, should examine why too often there are walls between us and our communities. We should be building bridges instead. We should find ways to celebrate the diversity that gives our city so rich a texture. Looking outward to Philadelphia's communities and inward at our own systems, we should try to learn why museums have not better reflected this cultural pluralism. We also recognized the need for help in learning about each other and about ourselves. And whatever we intended to do must have some fundamental connection to museums as informal educational institutions and should make use of their special "magic."

> We explored many possibilities and concluded that the unique strength of museums lay in the presentation, interpretation, and celebration of cultural pluralism.

What we learned during this initial phase can be summarized in three words: process, patience, and partnership. Process was crucial: the insights gained as we worked together were as important as the projects themselves. Since all this required time and attention, patience was also a prerequisite. And in sharing each step of the decision making, whether about the goals and objectives or the project's development, real partnership would be the key.

Getting Started

Portia Hamilton-Sperr

IN EMBARKING ON THE MUSEUMS IN THE LIFE OF A CITY INITIATIVE in 1990, we looked at Philadelphia's demographics, politics, and economic situation, as well as the cultural context. By the late 1980s the city was in disarray, local government was facing bankruptcy, and citizen morale was at a low point. To add to this malaise, traditional values were being questioned there as they were across the country. Issues of pluralism, diversity, multiculturalism, and "political correctness" had become hot topics.

Looking at urban demographics in America, we were not surprised to see Philadelphia's increasing pluralism. Since 1980, according to the most recent census data, the city's Asian population had more than doubled, to more than 43,000, and the Latino population had increased to about

By the late 1980s the city was in disarray, local government was facing bankruptcy, and citizen morale was at a low point.

90,000. According to a March 1991 *Philadelphia Inquirer* article, "the city is far less integrated than it was earlier this century. [In a total population of about 1.6 million] Philadelphia is 54 percent white and 40 percent black. Nearly three-quarters of the black population live on census blocks where at least nine out of ten people are black." An April 1991 article from the same

In considering what role cultural institutions might or should play in bettering our city at a time when problems were only getting worse, there seemed to be more institutional priority given to marketing than to social issues.

paper noted that "as segregation increases in cities such as Philadelphia, blacks in some neighborhoods lose touch with middle-class blacks who have moved to new and often suburban communities. . . . Networks among families and friends that formerly passed along information about job openings or other opportunities become frayed as a community becomes more radically isolated."

In considering what role cultural institutions might or should play in bettering our city at a time when problems were only getting worse, there seemed to be more institutional priority given to marketing than to social issues. This focus was driven by the very real and understandable need for financial survival. Many museums were, of course, still trying to address social needs in a general way. Most of them were providing subsidized admissions for low-income children. Many were working cooperatively with the public school system or had some kind of traveling programming. A few continued to mount special exhibits to attract nonmajority visitors. But few programs existed to meet social problems more directly.

Given all these factors, starting Museums in the Life of a City appeared to be an act of bravura, if not foolishness or worse—some kind of well-meant do-goodism.

I remember being met with thinly veiled condescension, or perhaps skepticism verging on cynicism. Although representatives from quite a few community groups and museums did see the initiative as a hopeful beginning, some were frankly unenthusiastic, saying they were "just trying to survive." A few expressed openly their frustration with what they perceived as an imperative to take on yet more responsibilities at a time when they already could barely operate. We also had to defend ourselves against the often-expressed idea that the initiative was merely a marketing ploy—a suspicion the community groups often voiced. Wasn't it just an "outreach" project in the traditional sense of bringing so-called "nontraditional visitors" into museums?

Nevertheless, we persisted. Through public meetings, museums had the chance to learn more about the social and educational priorities of different communities in the city.

Although representatives from quite a few community groups and museums did see the initiative as a hopeful beginning, some were frankly unenthusiastic, saying they were "just trying to survive."

Key among these priorities were keeping young people in school, training them for meaningful work, creating jobs, fighting violence and drugs, and struggling to improve housing and health services. We suggested that in the light of this educational process, each participating museum might examine what institutional resources it could offer a particular neighborhood or community to join with them in their efforts for renewal.

The initiative's planning committee set the following goals for the pilot projects. Each project must:

- improve the communications between Philadelphia's many different communities and museums in relation to needs such as education and the strengthening of community values
- demonstrate, through action, the opportunities museums have to serve diverse and often culturally unrepresented citizens—African Americans, Asian Americans, Latinos, and Native Americans.
- forge new forms of partnerships between peers (communities and museums) whereby community leaders and museum professionals share decision-making responsibility
- empower communities and museums to deal with contemporary problems through cooperative strategies that take advantage more fully of each other's existing resources

• promote the active participation of a broad spectrum of people from the community and encourage commitment by museum staff and boards to reflecting the city's cultural diversity within their institutions

• have as their intention, even while at pilot project level, the strong possibility of continuing the relationships

Forty-one groups submitted project proposals. Eleven received financial support based on recommendations from a panel of leaders in the field of community-oriented cultural programming. They were:

• two internship programs—one in science and one in the visual arts—involving high school-age youth in the leadership of activities with children

We suggested that each participating museum might examine what institutional resources it could offer a particular neighborhood or community to join with them in their efforts for renewal.

• three oral history projects concerned with the history of Philadelphia's first public housing development and the history of two different neighborhoods

• a research project to investigate local resources for learning about Cambodian culture

• an exploration of cultural themes in maritime history involving children and families of an inner-city neighborhood

• a series of African cultural arts workshops and events involving elementary school students

• a workshop series designed to facilitate the establishment of a community nature center, urban garden, and reference library

• drama and visual arts workshops related to an exhibition of paintings by a distinguished African-American artist and involving youngsters from a performing arts training program

• a program of family-oriented events and classes intended to promote crosscultural understanding among the people of an increasingly multiethnic neighborhood

Supporting the Partnerships

Cynthia Primas

WHEN THE NEWLY FORMED PARTNERSHIPS came together in their pilot projects, they began by discussing their hopes and expectations— always with excitement and often anticipating achievement that might have seemed overly ambitious to us. They might envision helping young people develop self-esteem and gain job skills. strengthening the work of museums, promoting community values, working toward cultural understanding on deeper levels, and on and on.

In trying to determine whether a group would be able to work well together, we looked for several factors. There was the matter of individual personalities, and then there was the group itself, which although composed of individuals was a dynamic whole. A well-functioning group can have its own spirit, and the environment it creates is capable of bringing about changes in the participating individuals. We were excited when we saw this happen, particularly when it brought together community and museum people who had never experienced this sort of exchange.

We encouraged them to find ways to use dialogue, shared resources, and collaboration to set the stage for more long-term relationships as partners while they worked together.

The staff of the initiative did not ask the partners to work toward preconceived objectives. Instead, we encouraged them to find ways to use dialogue, shared resources, and collaboration to set the stage for more long-term relationships as partners while they worked together on the pilot projects. We realized that this kind of freedom to experiment is itself a challenge, calling into question basic assumptions made by all the partners.

Anticipating the difficulties that our participants would face in exploring cultural differences, we decided not to impose a preordained organizational structure, although that might have made things seem easier. Instead, we suggested a monitoring system based on what is called "action research," a process that focuses on collecting data reflecting the group members' views of their own reality. In this process, those with a stake in a problem help define and solve it. Group members can use information they have generated themselves for the achievement of their own goals. Ideally, what results is a process that comes from within the group to affect their own behavior and decisions. The initiative staff were available to meet with any of the partnerships to support their efforts to move ahead, but we did not think we could tell them what to do. In our work we focused most on equality and on trying to bring together people with different values and ways of looking at the world to work on projects of mutual benefit.

I was touched by the note I received from one project participant: "Thank you for your warm support and gentle encouragement as we charted a course through multicultural waters to reach a strong and dynamic collaboration." This kind of response supports my conviction that product and process must go on together to achieve the desired results.

We focused most on equality and on trying to bring together people with different values and ways of looking at the world to work on projects of mutual benefit.

Working Together

Johnson Homes Oral History Video Project

JOHNSON HOMES TENANT COUNCIL, HOUSING ASSOCIATION OF DELAWARE VALLEY, FREE LIBRARY OF PHILADELPHIA

This oral history video project was a benchmark activity for the James Weldon Johnson Homes, which was the first public housing development to be constructed in Philadelphia more than fifty years ago. Through a partnership with representatives from the Free Library of Philadelphia and the Housing Association of Delaware Valley, Johnson Homes residents were trained in oral history research, video production, and tenant leadership. They planned a video featuring stories and reminiscences from older residents about the early years of their famous housing development—material that otherwise might have been lost forever.

While there had been many onsite social services and recreational programs in the early days of Johnson Homes, financial cutbacks and bureaucratic decisions eroded those programs and eventually led to their elimination, leaving residents with comparatively few cultural and recreational opportunities. Fortunately, however, strong leadership—particularly from Nellie Reynolds, then the Tenant Council president—enabled Johnson Homes to avoid the pitfalls faced by residents of many other developments. The oral history is their story: a story of achievement against the odds and of a tenants' rights movement to make public housing live up to their expectations for a decent place to live.

As part of the project, Linda Shopes, an oral historian from the Pennsylvania Historical and Museum Commission, provided training in oral history interviewing, and Scribe Video Center taught production techniques. Through their partnership with the staff from the Free Library and other professional consultants, residents learned historical research techniques—a valuable skill that also opened doors to the discoveries of maps and other materials that have increased their sense of pride about where they live. Many who had not been in the library since school days found much to attract their interest and to encourage return visits.

Reaching the Community through Peer Arts Education and Mentorship

PHILADELPHIA MUSEUM OF ART, TALLER PUERTORRIQUEÑO, CONGRESO DE LATINOS UNIDOS

This project provided paid summer internships to five Latino high school students selected by Taller Puertorriqueño and Congreso de Latinos Unidos and five college students chosen by the Philadelphia Museum of Art. The interns participated in an eight-week summer program to provide activities at the museum for several thousand children from inner-city camps and recreation centers.

The first three weeks were devoted to training the interns. They learned about how museums operate by meeting with curators and administrators, observing programs, researching aspects of the museum's collections, and visiting other museums in Philadelphia and New York. Amy Jared and other education staff members gave lectures and demonstrations on how to teach in the galleries and studios and how to write lesson plans.

During the remaining five weeks of the program at the museum, the interns were responsible for team teaching, teaching independently, and observing and evaluating each other. They had three special studio sessions to prepare lessons that they could take back to the community. They also had the chance to teach a printmaking workshop in the community with forty-five children from the Taller summer program.

Later during the school year, the five high school students met at Taller Puertorriqueño to prepare and teach their community workshops and plan a mural project for the spring. Alberto Becerra, a noted Latino artist hired as coordinator, took the students to Bryn Mawr and Haverford Colleges to see an art show, tour the campuses, and have lunch with Hispanic students. His objective was to increase the students' awareness of career possibilities.

In part as a result of this collaborative project, museum officials realized the possibilities for creating bridges to the community on a wider institutional level. Museums in the Life of a City inspired and made it possible for the museum, through its Department of External Affairs, to establish an institutional diversity program to apply the goals of the initiative in ongoing, permanent ways. Among the accomplishments have been sharpening the mission of the museum's Diversity Task Force, publishing a newsletter about cultural pluralism, doing an inventory of all works by African-American artists in the museum's collection, and reinstating the Community Network Project to cultivate relationships with African-American, Hispanic, and Asian community organizations.

Point Breeze Voices

ATWATER KENT MUSEUM, CENTER FOR INTERGENERATIONAL LEARNING–TEMPLE UNIVERSITY, POINT BREEZE FEDERATION, INC., POINT BREEZE PERFORMING ARTS CENTER

This partnership was formed to document the oral history of Philadelphia's Point Breeze neighborhood from 1920 to the present. Two-person teams were trained to interview present and former residents from different cultural and racial backgrounds living in the area. The material was transcribed with the help of the Atwater Kent Museum for use as the basis for a future music, drama, and dance production to tell the community's story. The project's goal was to help young people develop pride in where they live through exploration of their community's history. To promote the oral history concept, organizers of the project told the kids that "you own your own history. No one can take that away. . . . It is a privilege for you to be able to document and share your history with others coming up behind you."

The particular strategy of this project was to match young people and adults in interview teams. These two age groups learned together and in the process were able to develop a deeper understanding of each other. For instance, they attended a series of classes where they created "mental maps" of Point Breeze to become familiar with generational differences in how people perceive their surroundings. They also learned interviewing techniques from Linda Shopes, who had headed a similar oral history project in Baltimore. Four of the eight teams that participated in the training continued with the project and were able to amass forty-five interviews. Their taped interviews have been transcribed for future publication.

Although people of different ages were represented in the interviews, organizers were somewhat disappointed that they could find little ethnic diversity in their interviewees. Whites who had once lived in the Point Breeze area but who had moved away seemed reluctant to respond to requests to be interviewed. Project participants also noted a minimal response from the newer Asian residents of the area.

Yet despite adjustments to the original proposal, work continued. According to its organizers, a project such as this one requires more time and concentrated effort than originally anticipated. More recently, however, the neighborhood has begun to develop a small community history museum that will incorporate this earlier work.

Who We Were, Who We Are

NEIGHBORHOOD ACTION BUREAU, NATIONAL MUSEUM OF AMERICAN JEWISH HISTORY

This internship project was developed for several purposes: to create a base for collaborative research between the partner organizations; to offer intensive training to high school interns in writing, editing, and computer skills; and to begin to discover the largely unexplored history of North Central Philadelphia's Germantown-Lehigh neighborhood.

The materials collected focused on area schools, businesses, and housing projects. Long-time residents told about race relations, schools, gangs, and the changing relationships between Jewish Americans and African Americans in the 1960s. Interns contributed articles to the neighborhood newspaper, the *Community Messenger.* They created a file of materials for future use by the community, documenting the varied ways in which people experience social and cultural change.

Newspaper editor Len Zangwill listed approximately twenty long-time community residents to interview. He then published an advertisement inviting other local people to share their memories. Zangwill and Karen Mittelman from the museum worked with the interns to edit the transcripts of these interviews, identifying common themes and suggesting new questions that emerged.

When the interns became more engaged with the issues, they began to understand the terms in which people in the community frame their own social experience. A man who moved to Germantown in 1959 remembers when shops along Germantown Avenue sold expensive dresses from New York—"They were high fashion"—and notes that as the neighborhood changed and long-term homeowners left Germantown, "the trees left and green lawns left." Another man, a resident since the 1960s, describes the Germantown of his boyhood as the "heart of Philadelphia."

From the beginning, however, this project experienced participant turnover. High-school-age interns found it difficult to make a long-term commitment to a program of research and writing and to make this project their own. Both partner institutions underestimated the amount of staff time and energy necessary to build a collaborative relationship. Two interns, however, remained actively involved and committed to the project. In addition to interviewing community residents, they conducted research into the history of particular stores and local businesses.

Their work gave them a sense of how history is actually lived as well as how it is intellectually shaped and written by historians. Without question, the understanding of neighborhood change has been the most valuable outcome for all participants.

Neighbors in Caring

ZOOLOGICAL SOCIETY OF PHILADELPHIA, PARKSIDE DAY CARE CENTER, MANTUA AGAINST DRUGS

This partnership between the zoo, a major mainstream educational and cultural organization, and two West Philadelphia community groups was aimed at giving children challenging educational programming while providing a chance for zoo educators to strengthen their ties with neighborhoods and get to know residents person-to-person.

The project consisted of workshops at the zoo focused on setting up an urban nature center, a garden, and a reference library in the community. Programs stimulated problem-solving skills, group cooperation, and pride in taking responsibility for living things. The zoo staff saw their role as providing opportunities for greater awareness of the environment. They offered information about career opportunities in environmental and scientific work and represented role models for the children.

Zoo visits alternating with workshops at the Parkside location kept that center's children busy throughout the project. In sessions on topics such as animal senses, habitats, the basics of life, and food webs, children participated in games, songs, and crafts designed to reinforce educational concepts. The center's live animal collection was a popular part of the project, with children observing and participating in the care of the animals.

During the project, staff of the Mantua Against Drugs program noted that it was unrealistic to expect involvement by their population, which they identified as mostly low-income. They also observed that other programs offered through the Mantua Center competed for their children's time. So "Zoo Camp" scholarships were provided instead to young people from the Mantua area. Zoo staff concluded that the project could have been structured to ensure that all participants had the same expectations from the start. Paradoxically, as the largest of the three organizations, the zoo had been hesitant to assume leadership, yet the other organizations had made this unspoken assumption.

A community participant commented that "we all shared decision making, and our relationship is based on mutual respect. . . . The process was raggedy at first and tough going," but it eventually progressed well. The project weathered early communication and scheduling problems, arriving at a later reorganization to better meet the needs of the participants while still serving the original goals of the project.

Partnerships for Achieving Careers in Technology and Science (PACTS)

GERMANTOWN BOYS AND GIRLS CLUB, FRANKLIN INSTITUTE, NATIONAL SOCIETY OF BLACK ENGINEERS, NATIONAL ORGANIZATION OF BLACK CHEMISTS AND CHEMICAL ENGINEERS

This collaboration, an internship program that took place in the summer of 1991 with follow-up activities during the ensuing school year, gave twenty-five African-American high school students—both girls and boys—firsthand experience in the fields of science and technology while also strengthening their sense of self-confidence. It was a chance for these young people to get to know role models for possible future career choices.

As a key part of the program, professionals from various applied sciences were asked to join the students in a series of Saturday training workshops at the Franklin Institute that covered a range of scientific disciplines. With the help of these mentors, the students were able to develop lesson plans and teach younger visitors to the Franklin Institute during the summer. Later, they helped teach children in the Boys and Girls Club after-school programs.

The students were selected not only for their interest in science but for their desire to give something back to their community. Their parents' commitment to the program was another requirement. During the project, the students had the opportunity to use what they were learning to instruct others. They also visited their mentors' workplaces to become acquainted with what scientific and technical jobs are really like. The encouragement from home, community organization, museum, and professionals was the chief ingredient in the success of the project.

One of the organizers from the Franklin Institute, Kelly Woodland, noted in his report that "one popular misconception dispelled by our project was the idea that black parents are uninterested in their children's academic involvement. Through this pilot project we demonstrated the critical importance of having families supportively involved in the process along with the museum and the professionals who act as role models."

Explorations

To further an understanding of how the world's waterways have linked cultures and peoples from around the globe, the Maritime Museum in cooperation with the Parkside Association embarked on their own eighteen-month voyage of exploration and artistic expression.

A Delaware River cruise on the *Spirit of Philadelphia* introduced participants—young children and their families—to the maritime history of their own city and helped them learn firsthand the role of the river and the port in the life of their city today. Some sessions took place in the community, where artist Isaac Maefield and educator Bill Ward joined forces in hands-on workshops combining art projects with maritime lore. Other sessions introduced participants to the museum and the historic ship models and paintings in its galleries. In a special performance workshop, a costumed storyteller re-created life aboard an eighteenth-century sailing ship—the smells, sounds, and songs, the hardships, and the adventure of visiting exotic lands.

In classes at the museum and Parkside, students expanded their understanding of the types of ships used in different countries during the age of exploration—the African canoe, the Chinese junk, or the European galleon. In drawings, wood, clay, and collage they created their own renditions of these vessels. They discovered the importance of the spice trade and traced the voyages of European ships to the spice-producing countries of the world. Next, they imagined stopping off in Europe, Africa, or Asia and made masks reflecting the folklore and customs of these regions. These works were incorporated into an exhibition, *Folkways and Waterways,* which was on view at the museum for several months and later was used in the Maritime Museum's other educational programs.

On a modern-day voyage of discovery, the community participants discovered a new and unknown museum that lay beyond the boundaries of their familiar world. At first they may have found the museum intimidating, but soon it became a friendly home port, a welcoming haven. This Parkside-Maritime collaboration has provided a fresh perspective on the age of exploration which, according to the organizers, has been a benefit to both partners.

Cultural Interaction Project

AFRO–AMERICAN HISTORICAL AND CULTURAL MUSEUM, D. N. FELL ELEMENTARY SCHOOL, FELL HOME AND SCHOOL ASSOCIATION, SALVATION ARMY DAY CARE CENTER

The purpose of this project has been to enhance the understanding of African-American culture and heritage and to develop and strengthen the relationship among the participating communities. Dr. Eleanor Walls, principal of the Fell Elementary School, and her teachers worked with the museum's staff and consultants to implement a cultural program for the 500 children at the school involving music, crafts, storytelling, and films.

Programs were held frequently throughout the school year: six visits to the museum with special activities and eighteen cultural activities at the school. The project encompassed the celebration of Kwanzaa, Martin Luther King, Jr.'s birthday, Black History Month, Presidential Jazz Weekend, and a finale—the African Festival at the Fell School in April.

In a South Philadelphia school where half the children are non-African Americans from the neighborhood and the other half are African Americans bussed in by the Salvation Army, these programs—especially the festival—were an extraordinary way to learn about another culture through the arts, food, and traditional costume. A Ghanaian teacher, for instance, provided historical background on the lives of African people, and an African-American artist worked with the teachers to paint scenery and make artifacts for a play given at the festival. Several teachers found materials in the museum's bookstore to use in their classrooms.

The process of preparing the culminating event was particularly important in helping teachers, children, and parents understand and appreciate African-American heritage. Moreover, special visits to the Afro-American Museum and the family program of Jazz Live concerts have paved the way for a special continuing relationship with parents. Some of the most enthusiastic children took their families to visit the museum after their school activities. They were proud to play the role of museum "ambassadors."

The Afro-American Museum's staff also benefited from this collaborative experience. They intend to refine the program so as to continue implementing it in the surrounding school district.

Horace Pippin: A Model for Collaborative Interpretation

FREEDOM THEATRE, PENNSYLVANIA ACADEMY OF THE FINE ARTS

The collaboration between Freedom Theatre and the Pennsylvania Academy of the Fine Arts (now the Museum of American Art) involved people from the African-American community in developing the academy's exhibitions and public programming. Using the occasion of an upcoming exhibition on the African-American artist Horace Pippin (1888–1947), the two organizations cosponsored workshops to generate feedback from participants to be incorporated into the academy's educational materials and programs.

Students from Freedom Theatre's summer Performing Arts Training Program helped develop a workshop model for the African-American community. These students, ages nine to twelve, participated in weekly creative workshops—arts and crafts and drama—that sparked discussion about Horace Pippin's work. The arts and crafts sessions included student interpretations of some of Pippin's paintings using fabrics and other materials. Creative dramatic exercises gave the students greater appreciation for the artist and his work. One of the exercises consisted of dramatizing various scenes depicted in his paintings, giving the students a chance to understand both the thoughts of the artist when he was painting and the era in which he worked.

As part of the project, focus groups were convened with students who had participated in the workshop model, parents of other students in the training program, and the Freedom Theatre staff. Slides of Pippin's work were shown, and educators from the academy recorded the group's impressions. The responses led to suggestions for changes in the labels being prepared for the academy's exhibition.

This project gave some of the children from Freedom Theatre an opportunity to discover new and different aspects of the fine arts. Instead of "just looking" at a picture in the galleries, the students were figuratively able to "touch and feel" the artist's work. Project organizers anticipate that information generated from the activities of this partnership will enable future visitors to get in touch with and feel moved by the art they see.

Consortium for Community Interaction

AMERICAN SWEDISH HISTORICAL MUSEUM, SOUTH PHILADELPHIANS UNITED, CAMBODIAN ASSOCIATION OF GREATER PHILADELPHIA, LAOS FAMILY COMMUNITY ORGANIZATION OF GREATER PHILADELPHIA, INTERESTED NEIGHBORS CIVIC ASSOCIATION, JASON DOUGLAS DANCE ACADEMY

Six organizations came together to sponsor a series of family-oriented events through which different ethnic communities in South Philadelphia could learn about each others' cultural heritage. The first activity, a summer Festival of Nations, has taken place on the grounds of the American Swedish Museum for several consecutive summers, bringing together neighborhood residents to enjoy music, dance, and ethnic foods. In addition, a fall 1991 series of ethnic cooking classes held at the museum presented Swedish, Cambodian, Italian, and Laotian dishes, and a spring 1992 series of ethnic dance classes shared cultural expression, drawing people from the surrounding community. Participants were enthusiastic about the chance to learn more both about their own cultures and those of others in their increasingly multicultural neighborhood.

"I learned that everything does not have to start on time or run smoothly to be successful," said museum director Ann Brown. "We all learned how to work together, make decisions, and still respect each other's leadership and authority. . . . The museum now has strong ties with members of the local community and is slowly becoming a clearinghouse for information." For instance, the museum has "adopted" the Ware Public School, which has a large Asian American population. The contacts the museum made during its pilot project have enabled museum staff to put teachers in touch with the local Laotian and Cambodian communities.

Museums and Communities Speak

Cynthia Primas

DURING 1992, THE FINAL YEAR OF THE INITIATIVE, I developed an evaluation process that consisted of interviews with community people and museum people involved in running the pilot projects. The typical reactions of the community respondents were different from those of the museum participants. Community people are acutely aware of their vulnerability to the problem of scarce resources; their needs are immediate and practical. They often expressed mistrust of ambiguity or anything that they considered theoretical. Having no doubt experienced disappointment in the past, they seemed hesitant to express too much enthusiasm. They valued their person-to-person interactions the most. Only sustained actions, they said, earn their trust. Museum respondents expressed more professional satisfaction in what they learned through the projects. Some spoke of their own self-doubts and feelings of awkwardness in their interactions with their partners. Most concluded on an optimistic note.

While there was considerable agreement among the people I interviewed, I detected much greater skepticism from the communities than from the museums. Because communities have this wait-and-see attitude, museums will have to continue their efforts to strengthen the still-fragile bonds of trust if they are truly committed to change.

What do you think about collaborative relationships?

The museums respond:

It has taken a long time to get to be partners. I'm still learning new strategies.

The community really relied on us. . . . These partnerships require serious commitment, and the goals must be small and achievable.

Partnerships need more management than one would imagine! They involve role negotiations. They're a team-building process.

The community organizations respond:

Our communities have monumental problems. . . . Talents and skills need to come together, because the problems are bigger than the resources, which are shrinking. . . . But we must go in this direction or face a greater tragedy than we had in the Los Angeles riots.

People from communities will only collaborate when they feel it's something important to do. Otherwise, time and resources will be put into something more vital to the life of their organizations.

Museums have a different way of seeing things. We haven't known clearly what each other's investment is in the relationship. . . . Partners have to trust each other.

Partners must know their limitations. You can promise too much and not be able to follow through.

Did you anticipate resistance to your project?

The museums respond:

I was not particularly surprised that my museum did not embrace the concept of our pilot project.

I wanted to make my cultural organization "user friendly," but we had no strategies to help this along.

Creating something new is a slow process. Resistance gets down to us not really being familiar with each other's format and environments.

At first there was resistance from our community group, which tapdanced around their structure. They did not want to look as though they were less organized than us.

In our showing interest, we were looked upon by the community as "checking up" on them. Suspicion was more the issue than resistance. It took a lot to get to the "we are just folks" stage where things can work better.

The community organizations respond:

With dual leadership, misconceptions were created. There was confusion in some people's minds as to how to separate responsibilities—maybe this was resistance.

Our museum partner did not see it as an opportunity to communicate with the community. Lasting change was really not a priority for the museum.

We did not anticipate resistance, but we felt it was played out when the museum did not respond to some of our requests.

It took time for us to build trust. . . but we realized that eventually we could work out the problems in our collaboration on our own.

Do you think a training model for partnership might have been useful?

The museums respond:

Role negotiation and a sign-off for the team members would have helped. . . . We pulled back a bit to allow our community group to come forward. (But not setting timelines resulted in not being kept up to date.) Maybe a training course should have been a prerequisite to doing the project.

Some people get bored if they stay on process too long. That might have held people up.

The community organizations respond:

People should have known what to expect when they started the project. . . . We needed more definition of what each participant's role was to be.

The best training was when someone from the staff met with the groups individually and helped folks to learn ways to work effectively.

Lots of information and materials were given out. If people read them and participated, they should have felt comfortable.

Training would have helped the museums realize that the community-based organizations have a lot to offer the mainstream. They could learn how to serve the community and how to expand their scope.

What were the disadvantages of this initiative?

The museums respond:

It was hard to define roles and to move ahead. . . . Getting and keeping in touch with each other was difficult. . . . The process was extremely time-consuming.

What was funded was product plus process; when the product is completed, the process ends with it.

One year is nothing for a collaboration. We needed to start a year ahead. A partnership has to be for at least two years.

The community organizations respond:

The goals and models presented in our orientation sessions were not very clear to me.

The equal decision-making process really does not work.

While we understand that "diversity" and new and different markets are extremely vital for the cultural organizations, we don't think they will ever do programs out of altruism.

We felt as though we were being used as "guinea pigs" for the initiative's organizers.

What might have been done differently?

The museums respond:

Match the groups and have them get to know each other first. Then start the project. Allow more time for us to put our projects together.

There should be more cultural sensitivity training for everyone in the museum, because we continue to presume that we understand where the community group is coming from.

A structured vehicle and funding should be developed so we could continue to work together and the project becomes institutionalized within the museum.

The community organizations respond:

Our pilot project would have accomplished more if money had been placed in one of our organizations. We needed one lead group doing the planning. . . . One person clearly needs to be in charge.

The consumers were left out of the planning process. In giving out grants, it's important to pull in the most active planners from the community.

More money, more money!

What have been the most promising aspects of this initiative?

The museums respond:

The project forced our museum to revisit and reflect on our mission. We have always talked about objects instead of people.

We came with preconceived notions of who we serve. Our project helped us break those notions and understand that there are ways of taking what we have and making it meaningful to others.

It opened everyone's eyes to the idea that it is possible to work together with people who are different from themselves.

Our project introduced us to an audience that otherwise we would have had no idea how to reach.

It provided our own staff with on-the-job training to work with community people for the first time. . . . We know the real people now who don't visit our museum. These are the people we want to serve in the future.

The community organizations respond:

At the very least, we now have a base—a foundation for continuing to work together.

We know respect between a large cultural organization and a community organization can develop.

The advantage was exposure to another culture. Our project opened up avenues of communication.

The benefits we derived were having the resources from our partner and networking with other projects.

The greatest benefit was that of the future possibilities—that larger initiatives could emanate from this grant.

What insights have you gained from being part of this initiative?

The museums respond:

I learned a lot about different cultures, the mission of our museum, and what our staff thinks.

We became aware of the differences in the way grassroots organizations are organized, managed, and operated. . . . We each have had different realities when it got to managing the pilot project's activities.

You have to understand each other's framework to be able to talk each other's language. . . . For the community, the question is how much or how little control people have over their lives.

We have seen that in the community there is commitment and caring—an incredible commitment of volunteers.

No matter how good a relationship a community group has with a museum, that relationship has to be maintained. We have to keep going back again and again if we expect people to remember that cultural institutions have services available to them.

The community organizations respond:

It made me appreciate the resources we have here in our own organization. . . . I got a better perspective on the importance of arts organizations to the community.

It helped me understand the constraints museums are under due to lack of funding and what will happen if funding is cut.

It was a learning process that helped us to be open to new and different things.

The pilot projects aren't just about money—they're partnerships, and we wonder how we can follow up on those things that have taken place.

Some people thought that the grant money was the big thing. They didn't put all their effort into the project, . . . and that was counterproductive.

We came to understand the scope of change—what is required to create change, how slow it is, but also how little things can make a difference.

Strategies for Long-Term Partnerships

Jim Zien

MUSEUMS IN THE LIFE OF THE CITY evolved in response to the perception that Philadelphia's cultural institutions should and can play a larger role in fostering public appreciation of ethnic and economic diversity and thereby enhance the prospects for social harmony in the community. The premise of the initiative was that museums could most effectively pursue this goal by establishing education-oriented program partnerships with community-based arts and social service organizations. The opportunity to obtain grant funds served as the principal incentive to partnership formation.

In November 1994—two years after the pilot projects were completed—Public Placemakers convened three focus groups composed of (1) community organization representatives, (2) museum representatives, and (3) representatives of both. The focus group discussions revealed a wide range of assessments, pro and con, regarding the experience of forming partnerships, planning cooperative projects, and implementing joint programs.

The focus group participants were asked to address several key questions about the Museums in the Life of a City initiative:

(1) What factors promoted strong museum-community organization partnerships and productive outcomes, and what factors caused partner dissatisfaction and program difficulties in the formative stage? in the program planning and development stage? in the implementation stage?

(2) Do the present programs and services of the participants reflect the underlying goals of the initiative?

(3) Considering the experience and the participants' current endeavors, what factors encourage museums and community organizations to collaborate for the purpose of serving economically and socially diverse constituencies, and what factors constrain them?

(4) What strategies might AAM and the other sponsors of Museums in the Life of a City pursue in the future to foster mutually beneficial cooperation among museums and community organizations?

The first two focus groups discussed the planning, development, and implementation dynamics of their partnerships. The combined group talked about current planning, development, and programming practices that reflect the goals of the initiative. The participants represented many but not all of the original partners (see page 45-46).

All things considered, a majority of the community organization and museum representatives who attended the sessions said that their participation in the initiative proved worth the investment of time and resources. A museum staff member said: [At first] I thought it was taking too much time and that I should have delegated more responsibility. . . . And at times I was resentful because I didn't think the return was there. But in hindsight . . . I look at the little push it has given me to . . . continue—although it's hard work—to diversify our audiences [and] diversify staff [and] board membership."A community organization participant had a similar reaction: "I think it's a wonderful project that should be expanded locally and nationally. . . . The primary change I would make is to [allow] . . . more time . . . [for] coming up with shared visions, goals, and understanding of the time and commitment everybody . . . has to make."

Despite such positive views of the experience, however, lasting partnerships failed in most cases to materialize.

Influences on Partnership Formation and Success

In a few instances, an existing cooperative relationship between a museum and a community organization was the foundation for a project collaboration. More often, partnerships were forged by relative strangers introduced through the efforts of the initiative staff.

The motivations for investing time and resources in partnership development varied widely, from pecuniary to pragmatic to political to philosophical. In general, the strongest partnerships were built on objectives closely related to the central missions, core capabilities, and natural resources of the partners. The weakest alliances were those that pursued projects only tangentially associated with the partners' fundamental purposes and those that depended on imported skills and means.

Satisfactions and Dissatisfactions

The highly diverse partnerships evoked a wide range of positive and negative assessments. On the plus side, many participants credited the initiative with bringing together organizations that would not otherwise have collaborated for the educational benefit of people who would not otherwise have gained meaningful access to geographically or psychologically remote cultural resources. The initiative also offered the partners useful insights into their respective missions, capabilities, and constraints. Some partnerships helped launch continuing professional relationships between collaboration-minded staff members.

A number of community organizations learned about program development resources and techniques from their partners. In the words of a participant in the Johnson Homes oral history video project: "A couple of the projects called for in the grant brought people from Johnson Homes into the Main Library [of the Philadelphia Free Library] . . . to do research using some of the specialized departments . . . that were not available in the neighborhood library."

Staff members of some museums gained greater understanding of the needs and interests of poorly served constituencies by visiting the neighborhoods in which their community partners operated and by implementing neighborhood-based programs for the first time. At the beginning of the Johnson Homes project, for example, "several library staff came over and took a tour of Johnson Homes [and the community] garden, and the [residents] had prepared something special for them. . . . I know that those people had not been in a [housing] development before. . . . Maybe the concept hadn't seemed very attractive until they . . . met the [residents] . . . and walked the streets. . .[and] were given fresh tomatoes and eggplants. . . . It just felt very good."

One museum educator talked about the satisfaction of getting out into the community: "I spend so much time in the museum that to . . . deal with . . . students [outside] the school setting, [without] a teacher. . .and to deal [directly] with parents . . . was very satisfying. I figure I learned a lot more than I ever taught in that regard."

The partners' primary dissatisfactions with their experiences appear rooted in three basic flaws in the structure of the initiative:

(1) the dollar-driven constitution of more than a few of the partnerships;

(2) the short time frame that was allowed for partnership growth, program planning, and implementation; and

(3) the small allotments of project funding relative to the intensity of staff effort required to achieve partnership objectives.

These underlying problems bred partnership deficiencies in some key areas of project management: communications, decision making, and organizational capacity and commitment.

Communications

Particularly for partnerships consisting of organizations with no history of cooperation, establishing and maintaining effective staff contact proved difficult. This problem was especially acute for several projects that had early changes in personnel. Predictably, communications difficulties and misunderstandings multiplied in direct proportion to the number of partners involved.

Decision making

The terms of the project grants called for equitable sharing of authority and responsibility among the partners. In practice, some projects suffered from indirection because individual participants were reluctant to assume decision-making roles, while others struggled to resolve both real and perceived control issues.

Organizational capacity and commitment

Community organizations and museums expressed concern over the low level of commitment by partners. Two factors influenced these perceptions: (1) funding for the pilot projects represented a proportionately a much higher contribution to the finances of small-budget community organizations than to those of their (mostly) much larger museum partners, and (2) major staffing disparities between partners resulted in project teams populated by senior leaders of community organizations on the one hand and lower-level staff of museums on the other.

Amplifying the usual demands of collaborations, these structurally different relationships to the initiative sometimes caused community organizations to conclude that certain cultural partners valued their joint ventures minimally. Museums, by contrast, sometimes concluded that certain community partners lacked the capacity to sustain their project roles.

Partnership Continuity and Pursuit of Goals Today

Very few of the partnerships represented in the focus group sessions continue to function today. The primary reasons that they do not are lack of funding, "fit," and familiarization time.

Lack of funding

The availability of grants was the basis for many of the partnerships. Some projects achieved their objectives, while others fell short. The brief period of funding, however, placed a premium on program design, development, and implementation. Consequently, no group of partners had the luxury of time to plan strategically, even if the members had the motivation to do so.

After exhausting the grant funds (which sometimes failed to cover the actual costs of participation), most of the partnerships dissolved. The exceptions are a few relationships of previous standing, maintained through continuing staff communication. The Free Library of Philadelphia, for example, continues working with Johnson Homes. The tenants' association president and the branch library have cooperated to establish a reading center at the housing project. The director of Taller Puertorriqueño comments that "the communication between Taller . . . and the Philadelphia Museum of Art has been consistent . . . because one of the reasons that I became involved was to make the museum aware of . . . Latin American artists here in the city. I've been working [at it] for decades. . . . Now we do an annual event at the museum through the education program."

Lack of "fit"

Some partnerships revolved around objectives only tangentially related to the missions of the participating organizations. As a result, they faltered in the face of staff changes or competition for resources from more central organizational endeavors. One museum participant remarked that "often, institutions have to jump through hoops to get money for a project that [finally] doesn't fit within [their] mission. . . . They sort of fit square pegs into round holes . . . because money is so hard to find. . . . I think that is what [happened] with [our] project." A community organization participant agreed: "We were able to map out what the museum's benefit was going to be, but we really couldn't [figure out] our benefit . . . except that we're getting a piece of this funding."

Lack of familiarization time

Asked to recommend refinements to the design of the initiative, community organization and museum representatives agreed unanimously on the need for partners to become familiar with one another's programs, staffs, facilities, and audiences and to engage in team- and trust-building exercises before beginning program development.

Support for Successful Partnerships

In the future, what support strategies would foster long-term, educationally oriented relationships between museums and community organizations for the purpose of advancing esteem for social diversity?

Support for essential groundwork

The Philadelphia experience suggests that partnerships between museums and community-based human service organizations grow best in a firm ground of mutual knowledge and understanding. The groundwork needed to support successful program collaborations includes these key elements:

MATCHING THE MISSION

Partnerships should advance the fundamental missions of their partners in important ways. Participating staff should clearly articulate, openly discuss, and explicitly acknowledge the missions, program and service priorities, and partnership expectations of their organizations. The educational, social, and material objectives of partnership projects should relate closely to the capabilities of the partner organizations and to the expertise of the personnel who will carry out the work.

LEADERSHIP COMMITMENT

The leaders of partner organizations should formally and jointly endorse their partnership and participate personally in its planning, development, and implementation in more than token ways.

CORE STAFF INVOLVEMENT

Primary responsibility for partnership planning and management should rest with key members of each partner's core staff. Contract employees, interns, volunteers, and other nonpermanent personnel should play supporting roles.

TEAM BUILDING

Before attempting to develop and conduct collaborative programs, partner staffs should enhance their capacity to work together productively by pursuing formal or informal team-building. These experiences should include thorough familiarization with one another's programs, facilities, neighborhoods, and constituencies.

LOW-RISK EXCHANGES OF LEARNING EXPERIENCE

Partners' ongoing programs represent ready resources for a series of reciprocal learning experiences. Hosted in turn by each partner for staff and audience members of the others, these experiences can reveal areas of opportunity for collaboration and indicate potential sources of difficulty.

Support for progressive program development

Educational and cultural programs of real value to both audiences and sponsors most often evolve progressively, through several developmental stages—from concept and content development to program design, staff training, piloting, refinement, and full-scale implementation. For any single museum or community organization, the process requires a substantial investment of money, time, and talent. A collaborative enterprise makes even higher demands on participant resources. Consequently, program partnerships that lack a series of phased and methodical creation stages seldom succeed or endure.

The critical components of effective program planning and development include:

CLEAR ASSIGNMENT OF PARTNERSHIP MANAGEMENT AND DECISION-MAKING ROLES

The partnership as a whole and the individual partners must confer leadership responsibility and ultimate authority on capable, trusted team members. Approaches to resolving disputes among partners should be agreed upon in advance.

CREATIVE CONCEPT FORMULATION

The program concepts that a partnership pursues should represent the creative thinking of all team members. Professional facilitation of concept development discussions can prove worthwhile.

COHERENT CONTENT DETERMINATION

The content focus of a program partnership should emerge from a systematic consideration of each partner's relevant and significant resources as well as the needs and interests of prospective audiences.

MANAGEABLE PROGRAM DESIGN

The functional and logistical requirements of partnership programs should closely match the human, material, and facility capacities of the partners. These capacities should be assessed and understood in advance by all team members.

STAFF SKILL BUILDING FOR COOPERATIVE PROGRAMMING

The staff members who will develop and conduct the programs of a partnership must learn to work effectively across organizational (and possibly cultural) boundaries. Early in the planning phase of a collaborative relationship, the partners should seek a professional assessment of the most useful types of training for their joint purposes, in such areas as teamwork, creative planning methods, effective communication techniques, or cultural awareness. Time and funds then should be set aside to engage appropriate organizational and professional development expertise.

PROGRAM TRIALS, FORMATIVE EVALUATION, AND REVISION

Programs under development require trial runs in order to realize their highest potential. Partnerships must try out their program content and delivery methods, and they also must put their cooperative operating arrangements to the test. Provision should be made for a round of pilot programs followed by an assessment of strengths and weaknesses and execution of needed refinements.

Support for structurally innovative partnerships

The Philadelphia initiative offered support to museums and community organizations to undertake collaborative programs for constituents of the community-based partners. The short-term, product-driven nature of the partnerships was not destined to affect significantly the established purposes and regular activities of the participants. As an alternative, partnership projects might focus on developing permanent new structural relationships—relationships that fundamentally improve the participants' ability to serve socially diverse constituencies well in the long run.

Structurally innovative partnerships would, for example, facilitate frequent interaction among partner organization staffs; establish a visible physical or programmatic presence for each partner within the facilities of the others; regularly represent the existence and activities of the partnership in the public information disseminated by the partners; freely share administrative resources (such as mailing lists), where feasible and mutually beneficial.

Important characteristics of such partnerships include:

ACCESSIBILITY

The partners would devise a variety of mechanisms for making their facilities, resources, and programs well known and fully accessible to their respective staffs and audiences—in psychological as well as physical and economic terms.

HABITUAL CONSULTATION

As a matter of course, partner staff members would consult together about opportunities to incorporate one another's concerns into prospective programs and services while they are still in the planning and development phase.

MULTIPLE FORMS OF COOPERATION

Partners would experiment with ways to cooperate in carrying out a wide variety of activities, such as in-school and after-school programs, exhibits, performances, festivals, special events, and educational resource development and dissemination.

Summary

Museums in the Life of a City engendered diverse experiments in collaborative programming among Philadelphia community organizations and museums. The range and variety of the projects implemented by eleven partnerships offer many insights into the benefits as well as the hazards of such functionally mixed organizational marriages.

To the satisfaction of a majority of the participants, the projects afforded new and positive learning experiences to youngsters and adults who otherwise lack meaningful access to the educational and cultural resources involved. In addition, the planning and implementation process exposed museum staff members to the daily life, dedicated people, and diverse environments of urban neighborhoods previously known in name only. In a few instances, mutually rewarding contact has continued beyond the project period.

Less productively, more than a few of the partnerships rested on shaky foundations. Some lacked objectives central to the purposes and capabilities of the partners. Others lacked strong leadership. Several simply involved too many partners with diffuse interests. Challenged to plan and implement cooperative programs in a relatively short period with relatively small amounts of money, many such partnerships experienced difficulty maintaining effective communications and operations.

In the final analysis, the successes and failures of Museums in the Life of a City suggest that museums and community organizations can join forces effectively to address some of the educational needs of socially and economically diverse urban constituencies. To succeed, however, partnerships must evolve gradually, through successive stages of familiarization; functional relationship building; program planning, development, piloting, evaluation, and refinement; and, ideally, structural innovation. Accordingly, support for serious initiatives in museum–community organization collaboration must be well targeted, reasonably generous, and patient.

Epilogue

Portia Hamilton-Sperr

THE MUSEUMS IN THE LIFE OF A CITY INITIATIVE was concerned with change. Yet American museums, as custodians of materials related to people, happenings, and ideas our society considers important, are by definition conservative: They maintain values. Now, however, they are being challenged to reassess many of their traditional assumptions in the light of increasing demands for inclusion and participation by our pluralistic citizenry.

Over the past decade museum professionals has been exploring the direction American museums should and probably will be taking. A number of museums across the country have begun to put into practice a strong reaffirmation of the museum's central role as being both educational and social. But this role, however valid, is not going to be accepted without questioning by many working in museums. Only recently, with initiatives such as ours and others, have the full implications of these ideas advocating social responsibility been developed beyond some earlier efforts by a few visionaries. We knew it would not be surprising if some museums were to give polite lip service to these new ideas while continuing business as usual, and we expected that some community groups would feel justified in their cynicism about the "mainstream." Fortunately, between these extremes there is a wide but diffuse group of people from both communities and cultural organizations who consider positive change possible.

We are deeply grateful to all of the people from both communities and museums for what they have shown us and for their willingness to persevere. From them we have heard some important thoughts about collaboration, partnership, and building bridges:

• Build collaborations as two-way streets to promoting cultural democracy. Contrast this approach to the often commendable but limiting idea of trying to "democratize" traditional culture through outreach programs designed only by the cultural organizations. Pluralistic relationships involve everyone's active participation, not only in planning and governance but also in the cultural outcome that "adapts to social needs," to echo Dr. John Robert's presentation to us at our first public program. "Culture is dynamic, . . . building upon previous manifestations of itself in a process of endlessly devising solutions to old and new problems. . . . When we revise our concept of culture, other cultures are presented in realistic, sensitive, and responsible ways; we engage in an act of creating value that recognizes democratic and humanistic principles."

• "Work from where you stand," said Mamie Nichols of the Point Breeze Federation. Be willing to take incremental steps, while keeping the larger vision in mind—that a people's culture is vitally important in nurturing and affirming their sense of worth as human beings. To stay relevant today, museums must expand what and how they present the cultures of many other people they have not included before.

• "Consider education as everything that broadens the definition of reality, . . . for example, by increasing the urban minority youth's educational and career options, and. . .facilitating their belief that they are capable of high intellectual and career achievement," to quote from the Urban League of Philadelphia's 1990 report. Find ways to link practical training to the museum's context as a meeting ground for ideas and intellectual inquiry. Show how firsthand encounters with objects, along with related experiences, can inspire curiosity, questioning, critical thinking, reflection, and esthetic appreciation so as to improve the chance of finding a better job, as well as enriching a lifetime.

• Respect the process of positive change as much as the product. Trust must be earned on a person-to-person basis over time. Some projects might have benefited from a needs assessment process, others asked for sensitivity training, while still others just decided to launch into their activities together. Dialogue may involve finding flexible alternatives or renegotiating previous understandings just as much as discussing more abstract issues like cultural pluralism.

• Expect to put money and resources as well as time into the work of building toward a pluralistic future, if that is truly a priority. Otherwise, the more immediate needs for funding to operate will crowd out the good intentions for change expressed by both the museums and the community-based organizations.

• "Begin and continue," was the essence of what a number of people told us. Although these pilot projects tried quite a few productive strategies, none could be considered the blueprint for future success. Having strong personal commitment to an idea or a set of accomplishments, however, was an important factor in the most promising cases. But these projects are only a beginning. Not to continue to nurture each potential relationship would only confirm the skepticism we so often heard expressed. As one museum representative commented, "We have to keep going back again and again if we expect people to remember that cultural institutions have services available to them."

Participants

Museums in the Life of a City
The Philadelphia Initiative for Cultural Pluralism

COCHAIRS

Joel N. Bloom, President Emeritus, Franklin Institute Science Museum
Robert W. Sorrell, President, Urban League of Philadelphia

PROJECT STAFF

Portia Hamilton-Sperr, Project Director
Cynthia Primas, Assistant Project Director

EXECUTIVE COMMITTEE

John Alviti, Atwater Kent Museum
Frances Aulston, West Philadelphia Cultural Alliance
Cheryl McClenney-Brooker, Philadelphia Museum of Art
The Rev. Jesse Brown
Rusanne Bucci
Lucinda Clark
Juvencio Gonzalez, Department of Puerto Rican Community Affairs
Sam Gubins, Academy of Natural Sciences
Ann Mintz, Franklin Institute
Patrick Murphy, Institute of Contemporary Art
Samien Nol, Southeast Asian Mutual Assistance Associations Coalition
Rowena Stewart, Afro-American Historical and Cultural Museum
Gail Tomlinson, Citizens' Committee on Public Education
Frances Walker, Parents Against Drugs

MUSEUM COMMITTEE

Academy of Natural Sciences
Afro-American Historical and Cultural Museum
American Swedish Historical Museum
Atwater Kent Museum
Balch Institute for Ethnic Studies
Fairmount Park Council for Historic Sites
Franklin Institute
Free Library of Philadelphia
Historic Germantown Preserved, Inc.
Historical Society of Pennsylvania
Independence National Historical Park
Morris Arboretum of the University of Pennsylvania
National Museum of American Jewish History
Pennsylvania Academy of the Fine Arts
Philadelphia Maritime Museum
Philadelphia Mummers Museum
Philadelphia Museum of Art
Please Touch Museum
Rosenbach Museum and Library
University of Museum of Archaeology and Anthropology
Zoological Society of Philadelphia

FOCUS GROUP PARTICIPANTS, NOVEMBER 1994

Community organizations group

Boys and Girls Club of Germantown
Freedom Theatre
Interested Neighbors Civic Association
Johnson Homes Tenant Council
Parkside Community Center
Philadelphia Housing Authority
Point Breeze Federation
Point Breeze Performing Arts Center
Taller Puertorriqueño

Cultural institutions group

Afro-American Historical and Cultural Museum
Center for Intergenerational Learning, Temple University
Franklin Institute Science Museum
Free Library of Philadelphia
Philadelphia Maritime Museum
Philadelphia Museum of Art
Philadelphia Zoo

Combined group
Citizens' Committee on Public Education
Congreso de Latinos Unidos
Free Library of Philadelphia
National Museum of American Jewish History
Pennsylvania Academy of the Fine Arts, Museum of American Art
Philadelphia Housing Authority
Philadelphia Maritime Museum
Philadelphia Museum of Art
Point Breeze Performing Arts Center
West Philadelphia Cultural Alliance

AMERICAN ASSOCIATION OF MUSEUMS

The American Association of Museums (AAM) is the national service organization representing museums and museum professionals. Since its founding in 1906, the association has been dedicated to promoting excellence within the museum community and to providing a variety of services to the nation's museums and their staffs. AAM is also the national accrediting body for museums and serves as a national voice for museums through an active government affairs program. As such, it is the focal point for the major issues facing museums in our country today.

PARTNERS FOR LIVABLE COMMUNITIES

Partners for Livable Communities (formerly Partners for Livable Places) is a nonprofit organization dedicated to improving the quality of life and social equity in communities through the use of cultural and natural resources. Its programs cultivate local leadership networks for community advancement. Partners' initiative, "Shaping Growth in American Communities," in which Museums in the Life of a City has been a participant, is a four-year program involving more than fifty American cities and towns.

PEW CHARITABLE TRUSTS

The Pew Charitable Trusts, a national and international philanthropy with a special commitment to Philadelphia, support nonprofit activities in the areas of conservation and the environment, culture, education, health and human services, public policy, and religion. Through their grant making, the Trusts seek to encourage individual development and personal achievement, crossdisciplinary problem solving, and innovative, practical approaches to meet the changing needs of society.

CONTRIBUTORS

Portia Hamilton-Sperr, project director for Museums in the Life of a City, has a lengthy track record in the cultural life of Philadelphia. She was the founding director of Please Touch Museum from 1975 to 1988. She is a past president of the Greater Philadelphia Cultural Alliance and former chairman of the Mayor's Cultural Advisory Council.

Ann Mintz is director of special projects and planning at the Orlando Science Center, Orlando, Fla. As special projects director at Philadelphia's Franklin Institute Science Museum, she was a member of the executive committee for the Museums in the Life of a City initiative.

Cynthia Primas, assistant project director, is an independent consultant doing training for non-profit organizations in the areas of diversity, team building, leadership, and other aspects of organizational development.

Jim Zien is the principal of Public Placemakers, a multidisciplinary planning and project management practice in Cambridge, Mass., that provides leadership for educational, cultural, and community development.